GOOGLE'S IMAGEN 3
Inside the AI Canvas – Everything You Need to Know

The Game-Changing Artificial Intelligence Image Generator You Must See!

J. Andy Peters

Table of Contents

Introduction

Imagine a world where creativity no longer feels like a privilege reserved for the skilled or the trained. A place where a simple sentence, like "a glowing lantern floating across a starry lake," can spark life into a breathtaking image that looks as if it were crafted by the hands of a seasoned artist. This isn't some distant future. It's here, and it's called Imagen 3.

Google's Imagen 3 is not just another innovation in artificial intelligence; it's a glimpse into how technology can redefine the creative process. At its essence, it takes written descriptions—no matter how simple or elaborate—and transforms them into detailed visuals that feel almost tangible. It's fast, precise, and so versatile that it's equally suited for an artist shaping a bold concept or someone simply curious about what a "rainbow forest" might look like.

This book is your guide to understanding what makes Imagen 3 such a groundbreaking tool. It's about more than the technology; it's about what it means for creativity, for industries, and for the everyday person. We'll uncover how Imagen 3 works, how it opens doors for people who never thought they could create art, and how it pushes the boundaries of imagination.

At the same time, this journey isn't just about celebrating its capabilities. The power of such tools comes with a set of challenges and questions. Who owns AI-generated art? How do we ensure fairness in a tool trained on data from a complex world? And how do we balance the benefits of democratizing creativity with the responsibilities that come with it?

As you turn these pages, you'll find yourself diving into a narrative about speed, precision, and the potential to change how we think about creativity itself. Imagen 3 is more than just a tool; it's a story of transformation—one that's only just begun.

Chapter 1: The Rise of AI Image Generators

There was a time when creativity felt like it belonged solely to those who could wield a brush, compose a melody, or string words together in poetry. Over the decades, however, technology began to bridge the gap between imagination and execution. It started with rudimentary tools—early graphic design software, basic photo editing programs—each one lowering the barriers for those who wanted to create but didn't have traditional skills. Then came the era of AI, a force that would take creativity to heights few could have anticipated.

Artificial intelligence began modestly, learning to process images and recognize patterns. Early attempts at AI-generated art were clunky, almost laughable. Images lacked coherence, and the results felt more like experiments than breakthroughs. But as machine learning evolved, so did the ability of AI to mimic and eventually innovate within the boundaries of human creativity. Programs could now generate music, write stories, and even produce visual art. Each iteration grew more sophisticated, narrowing the gap between human intent and machine execution.

In today's fast-paced world, the demand for custom, high-quality visuals has skyrocketed. Content creation is no longer the domain of artists alone—it's essential for marketers, educators, and entrepreneurs alike. People need images that are unique, compelling, and tailored to their exact needs, often with little time or budget to spare. This is where tools like Imagen 3 step in.

Unlike its predecessors, Imagen 3 simplifies what once felt impossible. Instead of spending hours searching for the perfect stock image or hiring a professional illustrator, anyone can input a few descriptive words and receive a visual representation tailored to their vision. The ability to create without limits or prerequisites speaks directly to the needs of a society that values efficiency and creativity in equal measure.

Imagen 3 is more than a tool for professionals; it's an enabler for anyone with an idea to bring it to life. In a world where visuals dominate communication—on social media, in advertising, or even in classrooms—the power to generate stunning, meaningful images has become not just useful but essential. By giving this capability to everyone, Imagen 3 represents a turning point in the evolution of creative technology, making artistry not just accessible but universal.

Artificial intelligence has come a long way in turning text into images, but not all tools have evolved equally. Earlier models laid the groundwork, demonstrating that machines could interpret descriptions and attempt to create visuals. However, their limitations were clear—simple prompts often yielded images that lacked detail, coherence, or a true reflection of the user's intent. Faces were distorted, colors bled into one another, and the results were more fascinating for their novelty than their quality.

Imagen 3 is a leap forward, setting itself apart from its predecessors and competitors by mastering the art of nuance. Earlier models often struggled with complex prompts or requests that required an understanding of subtleties, such as lighting, textures, or spatial arrangements. Imagen 3 not only handles these with finesse but does so at a level that feels intuitive. A prompt like "a cat lounging on a sunlit windowsill, surrounded by blooming flowers" doesn't just yield a generic image of a cat and some flowers—it delivers a lifelike scene, complete with soft shadows, vibrant blooms, and the warm glow of sunlight.

While competitors like DALL-E or MidJourney have carved out their niches in the AI image generation space, Imagen 3 distinguishes itself by its precision and speed. DALL-E, for instance, is known for its creativity and ability to produce imaginative outputs, but it can sometimes sacrifice realism in favor of artistic flair. MidJourney, on the other hand, leans heavily into artistic styles, excelling in abstract and surreal interpretations. Imagen 3, however, strikes a balance—it's not just about generating imaginative visuals; it's about crafting them with a lifelike quality that feels grounded in reality.

What truly sets Imagen 3 apart is its approach to accessibility. While some tools require steep learning curves or technical expertise, Imagen 3 is built for everyone. The simplicity of its interface and the speed of its processing make it an approachable option for casual users and professionals alike. This democratization of creativity ensures that anyone, regardless of their technical background, can turn a fleeting idea into a vivid image.

The "text-to-image" revolution is more than just a technological breakthrough; it's a shift in how we think about creating. Imagen 3 embodies this shift, proving that the gap between thought and execution can be bridged in mere seconds, allowing imagination to flow freely and without barriers.

Chapter 2: Behind the Curtain – How Imagen 3 Works

The latent diffusion model might sound complex, but its essence is surprisingly straightforward. Imagine starting with a messy, abstract canvas—a swirl of random colors and patterns. The AI, equipped with the latent diffusion model, gradually refines this chaos into a clear, detailed image based on the description you provide. It's like sculpting a block of marble into a masterpiece, bit by bit, until every detail aligns with your vision.

Here's how it works in simple terms. When you type a description into Imagen 3, the system doesn't immediately conjure an image from scratch. Instead, it begins with a noisy or blurred representation, almost like a foggy photo. This initial state acts as a foundation, giving the AI a starting point. Through a process of iterations, it refines this blurry base, step by step, removing "noise" and adding details that align with the prompt.

The first step is to understand the text prompt. Imagen 3 uses advanced natural language processing to break down your words and interpret their meaning. Every detail you provide—colors, lighting, objects, or even artistic styles—is analyzed and mapped out. For example, if your prompt is "a glowing lantern floating on a lake under a starlit sky," the system identifies key components: the lantern, the lake, the stars, and the overall mood.

Once the text is processed, the AI enters the generation phase. The noisy base image is created, and the latent diffusion model begins its refinement process. Each iteration brings the image closer to clarity, guided by the detailed understanding of your text. The model applies its knowledge of textures, lighting, and spatial relationships to ensure the final output feels cohesive and realistic. The glowing effect of the lantern, the gentle ripples in the water, and the subtle sparkle of the stars are all fine-tuned as the image takes shape.

The latent diffusion model stands out because of its balance between speed and precision. Unlike earlier methods that either took too long or compromised on quality, this model delivers high-resolution, lifelike visuals in seconds. It's this efficiency that makes Imagen 3 not just a powerful tool but an accessible one, allowing users to create with ease and confidence.

By the time the image is complete, it feels less like a product of algorithms and more like a direct manifestation of your imagination. This seamless blend of technology and creativity is what sets Imagen 3 apart, transforming how we think about art and innovation.

Imagen 3 doesn't just generate images; it breathes life into them by mastering the intricate details that make visuals feel authentic. Elements like lighting, textures, and shadows are what separate a passable image from one that feels genuinely lifelike, and Imagen 3 excels at capturing these complexities with remarkable precision.

When it comes to lighting, the AI goes beyond simply brightening or darkening areas. It understands how light interacts with objects in the real world—how it bends around edges, reflects off surfaces, and creates depth through highlights and shadows. For instance, if your prompt describes "a candlelit dinner in a rustic cabin," Imagen 3 doesn't just add a generic glow. It simulates the flickering effect of candlelight, the soft illumination on wooden beams, and the warm ambiance that fills the space, making the scene feel as if it were plucked from reality.

Textures are another area where Imagen 3 shines. Whether it's the rough bark of a tree, the smooth gloss of ceramic, or the soft folds of fabric, the model pays close attention to these subtleties. This is achieved by analyzing patterns and materials in its training data, then applying that knowledge to create textures that feel tangible. A description like "a vintage leather-bound book" will yield an image where you can almost feel the worn creases and the rich grain of the leather.

Shadows, often overlooked in image generation, are critical for realism, and Imagen 3 handles them with finesse. It understands the direction and intensity of light in the scene, creating shadows that fall naturally and interact with other elements. A prompt featuring "a cat lounging by a sunny window" will include not just the cat's shadow but also subtle details like the soft diffusion of light through curtains or the interplay of light and dark on the cat's fur.

What makes this level of detail possible is Imagen 3's ability to balance speed and accuracy. Traditional models often had to choose between one or the other—high-quality images took longer to process, and faster models sacrificed realism. Imagen 3's technical breakthroughs eliminate this trade-off. It uses optimized algorithms to rapidly refine images through its latent diffusion model, delivering results that are both precise and timely.

This speed doesn't just cater to professionals on tight deadlines; it also makes the tool more accessible for everyday users. Whether you're brainstorming visuals for a campaign or simply experimenting with creative ideas, Imagen 3 ensures you get high-quality results without the wait. The harmony between its speed and attention to detail redefines what's possible in AI-generated art, opening the door to a future where imagination has no limits.

Chapter 3: Features That Make Imagen 3 a Game-Changer

Imagen 3 redefines what it means to create high-resolution visuals, delivering crisp, detailed images in mere seconds. In the past, achieving such quality required hours of work, whether by skilled designers or previous-generation AI tools that often struggled to balance clarity and speed. Imagen 3 changes the game by producing visuals that are not just fast but also strikingly lifelike, meeting professional-grade standards effortlessly.

The process begins with its advanced algorithms, which are designed to handle intricate details and maintain clarity even at higher resolutions. Whether it's the subtle veins on a leaf or the intricate pattern of a tiled floor, Imagen 3 ensures no detail is lost. This capability makes it an invaluable tool for professionals who need images for presentations, marketing campaigns, or other applications where quality is non-negotiable. For casual users, it offers a seamless way to bring their ideas to life with a level of detail they might never have thought possible.

But speed is only part of the equation. Imagen 3's true brilliance lies in its ability to understand and execute nuanced prompts with surprising accuracy. Earlier AI models often stumbled over prompts with multiple elements or abstract ideas, producing results that missed the mark. Imagen 3, however, processes language with remarkable depth, analyzing every word and its context to ensure the final output aligns with the user's intent.

For example, a prompt like "a golden retriever sitting on a red blanket in a forest during autumn" requires the AI to juggle multiple elements: the dog, its pose, the texture and color of the blanket, the backdrop of autumn foliage, and the overall composition. Imagen 3 not only captures each of these details but also harmonizes them into a cohesive image that feels thoughtfully composed.

This enhanced comprehension extends to abstract and creative ideas as well. A request like "an ethereal city floating among the clouds, lit by soft, glowing lanterns" challenges the AI to go beyond realism and tap into imaginative artistry. Imagen 3 rises to the occasion, generating visuals that feel both otherworldly and meticulously crafted, proving its ability to cater to a wide spectrum of creative needs.

The combination of high-resolution output and nuanced understanding makes Imagen 3 a standout in the world of AI image generation. It's not just about speed or precision individually; it's about how seamlessly the two come together to empower users to create without compromise.

Imagen 3 is a chameleon in the world of AI image generation, effortlessly adapting to a wide range of creative needs. Whether you're envisioning a photorealistic landscape that looks like it could hang in an art gallery or an abstract swirl of colors that feels like a page from a dream journal, Imagen

3 delivers with precision and style. This versatility is one of its defining features, setting it apart as a tool that doesn't just follow instructions—it interprets and enhances them.

For those seeking photorealism, Imagen 3 excels in crafting images that rival professional photography. A prompt like "a snow-covered cabin nestled in a pine forest under the northern lights" results in an image so detailed you can almost feel the chill in the air and see the auroras ripple across the sky. The AI captures nuances like the texture of snow on wooden beams or the glow of light spilling out from frosted windows, making the scene come alive with vivid accuracy.

On the other hand, if the goal is abstract art, Imagen 3 steps into the realm of imagination without hesitation. A request like "a burst of vibrant colors merging into the shape of a phoenix" produces a visual that defies reality while maintaining a sense of harmony and intention. The AI interprets abstract prompts with a keen sense of balance, blending elements in ways that are both surprising and aesthetically pleasing. This ability to shift seamlessly between styles makes Imagen 3 not just a tool but a creative partner.

What makes this versatility even more remarkable is how it caters to both casual users and seasoned professionals. For casual users—perhaps someone planning a personal project or experimenting with ideas—the simplicity of Imagen 3 is a revelation. No technical knowledge is required; a few descriptive words are all it takes to generate stunning visuals, leveling the creative playing field and making art accessible to everyone.

For creative professionals, Imagen 3 is a powerhouse. Designers, marketers, and content creators can leverage its precision and adaptability to streamline their workflows, saving time without compromising on quality. Need a custom background for a presentation? Done. A unique visual for an ad campaign? No problem. The tool's ability to quickly produce tailored, high-resolution images makes it a reliable asset for professionals who demand both speed and excellence.

Imagen 3's versatility lies at the heart of its appeal. It doesn't matter if the vision is rooted in reality or born from pure imagination—this tool transforms ideas into visuals with an ease and accuracy that feels almost magical, ensuring that everyone, regardless of skill or purpose, can bring their creative visions to life.

Chapter 4: Accessibility and Democratizing Creativity

Imagen 3's availability through Google's AI Test Kitchen represents more than just access to cutting-edge technology—it's an invitation for anyone, regardless of background, to step into the world of AI-driven creativity. The AI Test Kitchen acts as a playground, offering users the chance to experiment with Imagen 3 and explore its potential without any barriers to entry. For those unfamiliar with advanced tools or hesitant to invest in costly software, this accessibility is a game-changer.

Being free, at least for now, adds to the significance. In a world where many powerful AI tools come with steep subscription fees or licensing costs, Imagen 3's no-cost access opens the door for a broader audience. It removes the financial hurdle, allowing students, hobbyists, and budding creators to test its capabilities alongside professionals. This democratization of creativity aligns with a larger vision: making powerful tools available to everyone, not just those with deep pockets.

The timing of its free availability is equally strategic. By offering Imagen 3 at no cost during its early stages, Google not only builds excitement and engagement but also gathers valuable user feedback. Each interaction provides insights into how people use the tool, what features they value most, and where improvements might be needed. This collaborative approach ensures that the technology evolves in a way that truly meets the needs of its users.

For casual users, this access serves as an opportunity to experiment without fear of making mistakes. The AI Test Kitchen fosters creativity by encouraging people to play, explore, and imagine. Meanwhile, for professionals, it's a chance to integrate AI into their workflows risk-free, testing its capabilities and assessing its value before committing to its use in large-scale projects.

This period of free access also has broader implications for how AI tools like Imagen 3 are perceived. By allowing anyone to try it, Google is helping to dispel the notion that advanced AI is only for tech-savvy experts or high-budget organizations. Instead, it showcases AI as an inclusive, versatile tool that can adapt to the needs of everyday users as easily as it meets the demands of industry professionals.

The decision to make Imagen 3 freely available isn't just a marketing move—it's a statement. It signals a shift toward a future where technology empowers individuals across all levels of skill and experience, enabling them to create, innovate, and imagine without barriers. In this way, Google isn't just offering a tool; it's shaping the way we think about access to creativity in a digital age.

Imagen 3 is more than a tool; it's a gateway to a new era of creativity, particularly for designers, marketers, and hobbyists who may have once been constrained by time, resources, or technical know-how. By making this powerful AI freely available through the AI Test Kitchen, Google has effectively lowered the barriers that often keep people from exploring creative technologies.

For designers, Imagen 3 removes the time-intensive processes that have traditionally defined their craft. Creating custom visuals, especially those tailored to unique projects, can take hours—or even days. With Imagen 3, generating high-quality, detailed images becomes a matter of seconds. Whether it's a sleek background for a branding campaign or a visually compelling concept for a client pitch, designers can quickly create and iterate without being bogged down by manual work or limited by stock images. This efficiency allows them to focus on refining ideas and delivering polished results, making their workflows faster and more dynamic.

For marketers, the tool is equally transformative. Marketing thrives on visuals that captivate audiences, and the ability to produce tailored images on demand gives marketers an edge in creating campaigns that stand out. Imagen 3 enables them to align visuals perfectly with messaging, whether it's an ad for a product launch or an engaging social media post. The tool's ability to interpret nuanced prompts means marketers can easily produce visuals that evoke specific emotions or tell a story, all without needing a dedicated graphic design team. It's creativity without the usual bottlenecks.

For hobbyists, Imagen 3 is a dream come true. Often, people who dabble in art, design, or creative projects are held back by a lack of professional tools or skills. Imagen 3 levels the playing field, making it possible for anyone to turn their ideas into stunning visuals. Whether it's crafting a unique piece of art for personal enjoyment or creating visuals for a community project, the tool gives hobbyists access to professional-grade outputs without the steep learning curve of traditional design software.

By making Imagen 3 accessible, Google isn't just offering a tool; it's encouraging exploration and experimentation in ways that were previously unimaginable. The simplicity of the platform invites users to test their ideas without fear of failure. The immediacy of results fosters curiosity, pushing users to try new prompts, styles, and concepts they might not have considered before.

This open approach inspires creativity across all levels of experience. It allows users to focus on the fun of creating, discovering new possibilities along the way. For many, Imagen 3 will be their first encounter with AI-powered creativity, and by making it approachable, Google is not just building a user base—it's shaping how people view and interact with AI as a whole. It's a tool, a teacher, and a source of inspiration, all rolled into one.

Chapter 5: Practical Applications of Imagen 3

Imagen 3 is a versatile tool that seamlessly integrates into the workflows of professionals across various fields, offering them the ability to create stunning visuals with speed and precision. For graphic designers, marketers, and content creators, it's a game-changer, transforming how ideas are brought to life and elevating the quality of their work.

For graphic designers, Imagen 3 is like having an ever-ready assistant that delivers custom visuals on demand. The days of hunting through stock image libraries or spending hours crafting an intricate design from scratch are over. With just a few descriptive words, designers can generate visuals tailored to their exact specifications. Whether it's creating a sleek logo mockup, a striking background for a poster, or an artistic concept for a branding campaign, Imagen 3 delivers results in moments. This allows designers to focus on refining and iterating ideas, freeing up valuable time for the creative process.

Marketers find in Imagen 3 a powerful ally for crafting tailored ads and campaigns. Marketing thrives on visuals that capture attention and convey messages effectively, and Imagen 3 excels at generating imagery that aligns perfectly with a campaign's tone and goals. Need an engaging visual for a product launch? Describe it in a few words, and the tool provides options that fit the brand's identity. Want to create a series of themed social media posts? Imagen 3 can generate cohesive, eye-catching images that maintain a unified aesthetic. Its ability to understand nuanced prompts ensures that marketers can communicate their ideas with precision and creativity.

For content creators, Imagen 3 unlocks new possibilities for storytelling. Visuals are a cornerstone of modern content, whether it's a blog, a video, or a social media post, and Imagen 3 delivers unique images that enhance narratives. A creator producing a blog post about futuristic cities can generate captivating visuals to accompany their text, while a YouTuber discussing fantasy worlds can use the tool to create imaginative backdrops that immerse their audience. The tool's versatility means that content creators are no longer limited by the constraints of their own artistic abilities—they can now produce visuals that match the depth and detail of their storytelling.

Across these professional use cases, Imagen 3's greatest strength lies in its ability to adapt. It doesn't just generate images; it generates images that meet specific needs and exceed expectations. By offering a tool that is fast, intuitive, and precise, Google has empowered professionals to elevate their work, turning creative visions into tangible results with unprecedented ease. Whether it's for design, marketing, or content creation, Imagen 3 is setting a new standard for what's possible in visual storytelling.

For everyday users, Imagen 3 opens doors to a level of creativity that once felt out of reach. It's no longer necessary to be a professional artist or have years of technical training to bring imaginative ideas to life. Whether it's designing a personalized greeting card, creating unique decorations for a birthday party, or adding a custom touch to a scrapbook, Imagen 3 gives individuals the power to infuse their personal projects with originality and flair.

The simplicity of the tool makes it particularly appealing for casual use. A parent planning a child's birthday could type "a cartoon-style rocket ship with colorful stars" and receive a vibrant image ready to be printed for invitations or party decorations. A student might use Imagen 3 to craft visuals for a school project, transforming basic presentations into something truly memorable. Even those exploring hobbies like journaling or crafting can use the tool to enhance their creations with bespoke visuals that perfectly match their vision.

This accessibility and ease of use have larger implications for creative workflows across industries. Imagen 3 is reshaping how businesses and individuals approach design, marketing, and content creation by streamlining the creative process. The traditional bottlenecks of brainstorming, sourcing, and execution are being replaced with a seamless flow of ideas turning into visuals in seconds. Professionals who once relied heavily on graphic design teams or third-party vendors can now generate high-quality imagery independently, saving time and resources.

For industries that rely heavily on visuals—like advertising, publishing, and entertainment—Imagen 3 changes the game. Agencies can prototype campaigns faster, experimenting with multiple visual concepts without the usual delays. Independent creators and small businesses, often constrained by limited budgets, gain access to tools that enable them to compete with larger players. This democratization of creative technology allows more voices and ideas to emerge, enriching the overall landscape.

However, the impact isn't just about speed or accessibility—it's also about shifting the creative mindset. Imagen 3 encourages experimentation, inspiring users to push boundaries and explore new possibilities. With barriers lowered, the focus moves from the mechanics of creation to the act of imagining and ideating. This shift is redefining what it means to be creative, blurring the lines between professionals and everyday users, and empowering everyone to turn their ideas into reality.

In many ways, Imagen 3 isn't just a tool; it's a catalyst for change, making creativity more inclusive and altering the dynamics of how individuals and industries approach visual storytelling. It's about giving people the confidence and capability to create, whether for personal joy or professional success, and that's a transformation with far-reaching implications.

Chapter 6: Navigating the Challenges and Limitations

Imagen 3 operates within a framework designed to respect ethical boundaries, particularly when it comes to public figures and copyrighted content. While the tool's capabilities are vast, its intentional limitations highlight a commitment to avoiding potential legal and ethical pitfalls, ensuring responsible use of this powerful technology.

One of the most significant restrictions involves the creation of images featuring public figures. Unlike some earlier or less regulated AI tools, Imagen 3 does not allow users to generate visuals of celebrities, politicians, or other recognizable individuals. This safeguard prevents the misuse of the tool for creating deepfakes or deceptive content, which could harm reputations, spread misinformation, or undermine trust in visual media.

Similarly, Imagen 3 places firm boundaries around copyrighted material. The tool is designed to avoid reproducing or mimicking works that are protected under intellectual property laws. For example, if a user requests an image resembling a famous cartoon character or an artwork created by a well-known artist, Imagen 3 refrains from generating it outright. These restrictions are crucial in ensuring that the tool does not inadvertently infringe on the rights of creators or diminish the value of original works.

While these boundaries may seem limiting at first glance, they encourage users to approach the tool with creativity and originality. Instead of asking for direct reproductions, users are prompted to describe scenes, styles, or elements in detail, allowing the AI to generate unique interpretations. For instance, instead of requesting a well-known superhero, a user might describe a "heroic figure in a futuristic city with glowing armor," resulting in a distinctive and original image that evokes the desired tone without copying existing material.

These ethical considerations also address broader societal concerns about the role of AI in creative industries. By setting clear limits, Imagen 3 fosters a culture of responsibility among its users, emphasizing that while the technology is powerful, it must be used in ways that respect individuals and uphold intellectual property laws. It's a reminder that creativity can flourish within boundaries, often leading to more thoughtful and innovative outcomes.

In a world where the misuse of AI is a growing concern, Imagen 3's safeguards reflect a proactive approach to ensuring that technology serves as a force for good. These restrictions not only protect individuals and creators but also help establish trust in AI-generated content, paving the way for a future where such tools can be widely embraced without fear of harm or exploitation.

Imagen 3's restrictions on public figures and copyrighted content don't mean creativity has to be stifled; in fact, they encourage users to think more inventively about how they frame their requests. By focusing on descriptive prompts and broader themes rather than specific individuals or copyrighted material, users can explore a world of unique possibilities while staying within ethical boundaries.

Workarounds often begin with reframing the request. For example, instead of asking for an image of a specific celebrity, a user might describe their general attributes—such as "a charismatic figure with sleek dark hair and a confident smile, dressed in a sharp black suit." This approach allows Imagen 3 to generate a unique visual inspired by the essence of the idea rather than replicating a real person.

Similarly, when it comes to copyrighted material, users can shift their focus to style or era rather than specific characters or works. Instead of requesting a famous cartoon character, they might describe "a whimsical animal character with oversized eyes and a mischievous grin, drawn in a retro 1950s animation style." By doing so, the AI can create something original that captures the desired vibe without crossing into protected territory.

These creative workarounds don't just help users navigate limitations—they also foster a more thoughtful interaction with the tool. Instead of defaulting to replication, users are prompted to dig deeper into their vision, crafting prompts that inspire entirely new creations. This process often leads to results that are even more engaging and imaginative than direct copies could ever be.

The significance of these limitations lies in the message they send about responsible use. By setting boundaries, Imagen 3 reinforces the idea that powerful tools come with responsibilities. These restrictions protect creators, individuals, and the broader public from potential misuse, such as intellectual property violations or the spread of misleading content. They also align with ethical considerations in AI development, ensuring that innovation does not come at the expense of fairness or respect.

Beyond their immediate practical value, these boundaries serve a larger purpose: they help establish trust in AI technologies. Users, creators, and society at large are more likely to embrace tools like Imagen 3 when they see that safeguards are in place to prevent harm. In this way, the limitations are not a drawback but a feature, contributing to a culture of ethical AI use that prioritizes creativity and respect in equal measure.

Ultimately, these restrictions challenge users to think differently about how they create, pushing them toward originality and innovation. In doing so, they help ensure that Imagen 3 is not just a tool for generating visuals but a catalyst for responsible, imaginative, and boundary-pushing creativity.

Chapter 7: Ethical Implications and AI Responsibility

Bias in AI-generated content is a challenge that has accompanied the rapid advancement of artificial intelligence, including tools like Imagen 3. AI models are trained on massive datasets collected from various sources, and these datasets inevitably reflect the biases, imbalances, or stereotypes present in the material. Left unchecked, such biases can influence the outputs, potentially leading to representations that are skewed or unrepresentative of diverse perspectives.

Google, recognizing this issue, has taken proactive steps to address bias in Imagen 3. Central to these efforts are safeguards aimed at promoting diversity and fairness in the images generated by the tool. This begins with the data used to train the model. Google has implemented stricter standards for curating training datasets, ensuring they represent a broad spectrum of cultures, environments, and identities. By diversifying the data, Imagen 3 can produce outputs that reflect a more inclusive worldview.

Beyond data selection, Google incorporates mechanisms to detect and mitigate bias during the image generation process. Imagen 3 is designed to analyze prompts in a way that avoids reinforcing stereotypes. For instance, if a user requests "a doctor," the AI strives to present a range of genders, ethnicities, and appearances, rather than defaulting to outdated or narrow representations. This conscious approach ensures that the tool's outputs align more closely with the diversity of the real world.

Transparency also plays a key role in addressing bias. Google has openly acknowledged the challenges involved in creating fair and unbiased AI systems, fostering a culture of accountability. By engaging in ongoing research and welcoming feedback from users and experts, Google aims to continuously improve Imagen 3's performance in this area. This iterative process is essential for keeping pace with the complexities of societal expectations and ethical standards.

These safeguards are not just about improving the tool; they represent a commitment to using AI responsibly. Fairness in AI-generated content ensures that technology can be embraced as a force for good, rather than perpetuating existing inequalities. It also reinforces trust among users, who can rely on Imagen 3 to produce content that is respectful and representative.

While the issue of bias in AI is far from solved, Google's approach with Imagen 3 reflects an important step forward. By prioritizing diversity in data, implementing bias-mitigation strategies, and fostering transparency, Imagen 3 sets a standard for ethical AI use. These efforts not only improve the quality of the tool but also underline the potential of AI to serve as an inclusive and empowering force in creative industries and beyond.

Imagen 3 sits at the intersection of creativity and ethics, offering unprecedented opportunities for innovation while raising important questions about ownership, originality, and responsible use. As AI-generated content becomes more accessible and versatile, the need to balance its creative potential with ethical considerations grows increasingly urgent.

One major concern centers around ownership and originality. When AI generates a visual, who owns the resulting creation? Is it the user who supplied the prompt, the developers of the AI model, or neither? The ambiguity surrounding intellectual property in AI-generated content has sparked debates across industries. Users may feel a sense of authorship because they crafted the idea and input the description, but the underlying technology is built on datasets containing works from countless creators. This blending of influences challenges traditional notions of originality, especially when AI outputs bear subtle resemblances to existing works.

These questions are not just theoretical; they have real-world implications. For professionals using Imagen 3 to create visuals for commercial purposes, clarity around ownership is crucial to avoid potential disputes or legal challenges. Google's guidelines, which discourage copying specific copyrighted material, serve as a safeguard, but they also highlight the importance of ethical responsibility among users. Creativity is enhanced, not diminished, by respecting the contributions of others and ensuring that AI tools are used to generate truly original works.

The potential for misuse is another pressing issue. As powerful as Imagen 3 is for positive applications, its capabilities can be exploited to produce misinformation or harmful content. The ability to generate lifelike images in seconds could be leveraged to create deceptive visuals, such as fabricated news events or manipulated photographs, that spread false narratives. This risk underscores the need for clear regulations and safeguards to prevent the misuse of AI-generated content.

Google has implemented several measures to minimize these risks. Imagen 3 cannot generate images of public figures or copyrighted characters, and its output is designed to avoid promoting bias or harmful stereotypes. However, the responsibility doesn't stop with the developers. Users must also approach the tool with integrity, understanding that the ease of creation comes with an obligation to use it ethically.

Balancing creativity with these ethical concerns requires a collective effort. Developers must continue to refine safeguards and foster transparency, while users must engage with AI tools thoughtfully and responsibly. By establishing clear guidelines and promoting ethical practices, it's possible to unlock the full potential of AI while minimizing its risks.

In this balancing act, the focus remains on ensuring that tools like Imagen 3 empower people to innovate and imagine without causing harm. By addressing these challenges head-on, we can pave the way for a future where AI enriches human creativity while upholding the values of fairness, originality, and trust.

Chapter 8: AI and the Future of Creativity

Tools like Imagen 3 are reshaping the creative industries in profound ways, offering new possibilities while challenging traditional norms. By making high-quality visuals accessible to anyone with an idea, these AI tools are redefining what it means to create. They're not just speeding up workflows or enhancing efficiency—they're fundamentally altering the landscape of who can participate in the creative process and how ideas come to life.

For industries such as advertising, design, and entertainment, Imagen 3 is a game-changer. Agencies can now prototype concepts in minutes, testing multiple variations of a campaign without committing extensive time or resources. Filmmakers and game developers can use AI to generate concept art or visual backdrops, cutting down on production timelines while maintaining high-quality outputs. Even smaller players, such as independent artists or boutique agencies, gain access to capabilities once reserved for teams with significant budgets and technical expertise.

Yet, this revolution comes with its complexities. At the heart of the conversation is the debate over whether AI tools like Imagen 3 are disruptors or democratizers of creativity. On one side, AI is seen as a disruptor, threatening traditional roles and practices within creative industries. Designers, illustrators, and other professionals may feel displaced as AI increasingly takes on tasks that were once their exclusive domain. The fear is that automation could devalue human artistry, reducing demand for skills that take years to master.

On the other side, AI is celebrated as a democratizer of creativity, opening doors for those who were previously excluded from creative fields. Imagen 3 doesn't require technical expertise or specialized training—it allows anyone with an idea to produce professional-quality visuals. This empowerment extends beyond individual users to small businesses, educators, and hobbyists, leveling the playing field and fostering innovation across a broader spectrum of participants.

The truth likely lies somewhere in between. AI tools like Imagen 3 don't eliminate the need for human creativity—they augment it. Designers can use AI to streamline repetitive tasks, allowing them to focus on higher-level concepts and innovation. Independent creators can experiment without the fear of wasting time or resources. The result is a hybrid model of creativity, where humans and AI collaborate to push boundaries and explore new possibilities.

As these tools continue to evolve, the challenge for creative industries will be finding the balance between embracing innovation and preserving the integrity of human artistry. Rather than replacing creativity, AI has the potential to expand it, offering tools that inspire and enable more people to create. By reframing the debate, we can shift the focus from what AI might disrupt to what it can enhance—a broader, more inclusive future for creativity where imagination knows no limits.

The emergence of tools like Imagen 3 is not about replacing human creativity but expanding its possibilities. At the heart of this evolution lies the concept of hybrid creativity—a collaboration where human imagination blends seamlessly with AI's capabilities. By leveraging AI, individuals and industries are finding new ways to innovate, combining the best of human ingenuity with the efficiency and precision of advanced technology.

Hybrid creativity opens the door to opportunities that were once unimaginable. For example, an artist might use Imagen 3 to quickly generate concepts, experimenting with styles, compositions, and lighting before selecting the final direction for their work. This frees up time for refining details or adding personal touches, ensuring that the human element remains central to the creative process. Similarly, a writer could use AI-generated visuals to complement their storytelling, crafting richer narratives that engage audiences on multiple levels. In this way, AI becomes a partner, amplifying creativity rather than diminishing it.

This partnership also sparks the rise of entirely new creative roles. As AI tools become more integrated into workflows, there's a growing demand for individuals who can effectively harness their potential. Roles such as "AI creative directors" or "prompt engineers" are emerging, where professionals specialize in crafting detailed instructions to guide AI toward producing specific outputs. These roles bridge the gap between human vision and machine execution, highlighting the value of those who can think critically and communicate their ideas clearly.

However, with these opportunities come challenges, particularly the potential for job displacement. AI's ability to perform tasks quickly and efficiently raises concerns about the future of roles traditionally reliant on manual creativity. Graphic designers, illustrators, and other professionals may feel the pressure of an industry that increasingly values speed and cost-efficiency. Yet, rather than making these roles obsolete, AI is likely to reshape them. The focus shifts from execution to strategy, curation, and interpretation—areas where human expertise remains essential.

For those willing to adapt, the rise of AI can lead to enriched careers rather than diminished ones. Professionals who embrace these tools can expand their capabilities, taking on more complex projects and exploring new creative frontiers. In many cases, AI frees creators from repetitive or time-consuming tasks, allowing them to concentrate on innovation and ideation. The key lies in viewing AI not as a competitor but as a collaborator, a tool that enhances rather than replaces human talent.

Ultimately, the integration of AI like Imagen 3 into creative fields represents a reimagining of what creativity means in the modern era. It's not a question of whether AI will disrupt the status quo—it already has. The real question is how we, as creators, adapt to this shift and seize the opportunities it brings. By merging human imagination with AI's capabilities, we stand on the brink of a new creative renaissance, one where the possibilities are as limitless as our ability to dream.

Chapter 9: Real-World Reactions and Insights

The initial feedback on Imagen 3 has been overwhelmingly positive, with users across various fields praising its speed, accuracy, and versatility. From casual hobbyists to seasoned professionals, many have been quick to note how this tool has reshaped their approach to creativity. For some, it's the immediacy of results that stands out; for others, it's the precision with which the AI captures even the most nuanced prompts.

Users often highlight how intuitive Imagen 3 is to use. Designers have commented on how they can generate a rough concept in seconds, refining their ideas without needing to invest hours into manual drafts. Marketers have lauded its ability to create visuals tailored to specific campaigns, giving them the flexibility to experiment with different themes and tones. Even those with no design background find the tool empowering, allowing them to explore creative projects they might have previously deemed out of reach.

One striking example of Imagen 3's impact comes from a freelance graphic designer who needed to pitch multiple concepts to a client on a tight deadline. Using the tool, they were able to create three distinct visual styles for a branding campaign in under an hour, a process that would normally have taken days. The client was impressed not only with the quality of the visuals but also with the variety of options presented, demonstrating the tool's ability to enhance both efficiency and creativity.

In the marketing world, a boutique advertising agency used Imagen 3 to develop visuals for a social media campaign promoting a luxury product. With a prompt as simple as "a sleek, modern watch resting on a marble surface with soft lighting," the team quickly generated high-quality imagery that aligned perfectly with their brand's aesthetic. The campaign garnered attention for its polished visuals, earning praise from clients and boosting the agency's reputation.

Content creators have also shared their success stories, particularly in how Imagen 3 has enriched their storytelling. A travel blogger, for instance, used the tool to generate custom illustrations for blog posts, crafting visuals that brought their narratives to life in a way stock images never could. Similarly, a YouTuber focused on science fiction themes used Imagen 3 to create unique, otherworldly backdrops for videos, elevating the production quality and engaging their audience on a deeper level.

These stories underline the transformative potential of Imagen 3. Users are not only saving time and resources but also pushing the boundaries of what they can achieve creatively. The tool's ability to adapt to diverse needs and produce professional-grade results has made it an indispensable resource for many, proving that AI can be a powerful ally in the creative process. For those willing to embrace it, Imagen 3 is more than just a tool—it's a gateway to new levels of inspiration and innovation.

The broader creative community has embraced Imagen 3 with a mix of excitement and intrigue, viewing it as a tool that has fundamentally changed how people approach visual creation. For many, the allure lies in the accessibility of the technology. Artists, designers, marketers, and even casual users are discovering that they no longer need extensive technical expertise or expensive software to create something extraordinary. The freedom to transform words into stunning visuals has unleashed a wave of creativity that feels boundless.

What resonates most with the community is how Imagen 3 democratizes creativity. In the past, many creative projects were limited by resources or skills—those without a background in design often felt unable to bring their ideas to life. Now, with just a description and a few clicks, anyone can produce visuals that rival professional-grade work. This accessibility has emboldened individuals who might not have considered themselves "creative" to explore new projects and ideas, broadening the scope of who participates in artistic expression.

The community also appreciates how Imagen 3 encourages experimentation. Unlike traditional tools that require a learning curve, this AI invites users to dive right in. The immediacy of results sparks curiosity and playfulness, allowing users to test different styles, themes, and concepts without the fear of failure. For professionals, it's become a tool for brainstorming and ideation, while hobbyists use it as a way to explore creative possibilities they hadn't imagined before.

Discussions within the community often focus on the collaborative potential of AI like Imagen 3. Many creators see it as a partner rather than a replacement, a tool that amplifies human imagination rather than competing with it. By handling repetitive or technical tasks, Imagen 3 allows users to focus on refining their ideas, pushing the boundaries of their work, and exploring new creative directions.

However, there's also a healthy dose of reflection within the community. Conversations frequently touch on the ethical and artistic implications of AI-generated content. Some worry about the potential devaluation of human artistry, while others celebrate the ways AI challenges traditional notions of what it means to create. These discussions are a testament to how deeply Imagen 3 has embedded itself into the fabric of modern creativity—it's not just a tool; it's a catalyst for dialogue and innovation.

The overall perspective is clear: Imagen 3 has unlocked a new era of creativity. It empowers individuals to explore, experiment, and express themselves in ways that were once impossible or impractical. Whether you're a professional seeking to streamline your workflow or a newcomer discovering your artistic voice, the creative community agrees that tools like Imagen 3 are reshaping what it means to be a creator in today's world. It's not just about making images; it's about making creativity more accessible, inclusive, and dynamic for everyone.

Chapter 10: What Lies Ahead for Imagen 3 and Beyond

As groundbreaking as Imagen 3 is, it represents just the beginning of what AI can achieve in content creation. Future models promise to build on its capabilities, delivering innovations that push the boundaries of creativity even further. These advancements will likely focus on refining the precision, versatility, and accessibility of AI tools, while introducing entirely new possibilities that redefine how we think about creating.

One key area of innovation is the ability to handle increasingly complex prompts. Future AI models may go beyond interpreting descriptions to understanding the intent, mood, and context behind a request. Imagine being able to input a narrative—"a stormy night, filled with mystery and tension, with a shadowy figure emerging from the fog"—and receiving not just a single image but an entire series of visuals that evolve with the story. This deeper comprehension could bridge the gap between visual creation and storytelling, making AI an even more integral part of creative workflows.

Another likely development is the integration of dynamic and interactive content creation. While Imagen 3 excels at generating static images, future tools may allow users to create animations, interactive graphics, or even 3D models with the same ease and speed. For example, a user could describe "a bustling futuristic city at night" and receive not just a single scene but a fully animated, immersive experience with moving lights, flying vehicles, and shifting perspectives.

Personalization is also expected to play a significant role in future models. AI tools could adapt more closely to individual styles and preferences, learning from previous inputs to better anticipate and align with a user's creative vision. This would make the experience feel less like using a generic tool and more like collaborating with a personal assistant that understands your unique approach to creativity.

Beyond these technical advancements, AI will continue to reshape the broader landscape of content creation by democratizing access to tools and opening new doors for innovation. As AI becomes more sophisticated, it will empower individuals and organizations to tackle projects that once required significant resources or expertise. Small businesses could design entire branding campaigns in-house, educators could create custom learning materials tailored to their students, and independent creators could bring ambitious projects to life without needing a full production team.

At the same time, the boundaries of traditional art forms will blur. AI tools will inspire entirely new genres of creative expression, combining human imagination with machine precision to produce works that neither could achieve alone. The collaboration between human and AI will evolve into a seamless partnership, with each amplifying the other's strengths.

As these innovations emerge, so too will the challenges of ensuring ethical and responsible use. Questions about ownership, bias, and the authenticity of AI-generated content will remain at the forefront of the conversation, prompting developers, users, and policymakers to navigate this evolving landscape carefully.

In the end, the future of AI in content creation isn't just about making tools faster or more powerful—it's about redefining what's possible. By continuing to push the boundaries of creativity, AI promises to not only transform industries but also inspire individuals to imagine and create in ways that were once beyond their reach. It's an exciting frontier, and we've only just begun to explore its potential.

As tools like Imagen 3 continue to revolutionize the creative landscape, the need for balance between innovation and regulation becomes increasingly vital. On one hand, AI empowers individuals and industries with unprecedented creative capabilities, pushing the boundaries of what's possible in content creation. On the other, it introduces challenges—questions of ownership, ethics, and misuse—that demand thoughtful oversight.

Regulation plays a key role in maintaining this balance. Clear guidelines are essential to ensure that AI tools are used responsibly, safeguarding against the potential for harm. This includes protecting intellectual property, preventing the spread of misinformation, and addressing biases in AI outputs. By setting ethical standards, developers and policymakers can foster an environment where innovation thrives while minimizing risks to individuals, industries, and society as a whole.

However, regulation must not stifle the creative potential of AI. Striking the right balance means crafting policies that encourage experimentation and growth while maintaining accountability. Collaboration between developers, users, and regulators will be critical in shaping a framework that supports responsible use without hindering progress. Transparency, particularly in how AI models are trained and how outputs are generated, will be a cornerstone of building trust and fostering ethical practices.

For users, this is a call to action: explore tools like Imagen 3 with both curiosity and responsibility. The power of AI lies not just in what it can create, but in how it's used. By approaching AI-generated content with integrity—respecting the rights of others, avoiding harmful applications, and contributing to a culture of fairness—users can help set a positive precedent for the role of AI in creative industries.

It's also an invitation to push boundaries thoughtfully. Imagen 3 offers a unique opportunity to experiment, innovate, and bring ideas to life in ways that were once unimaginable. But with this power comes the responsibility to ensure that creativity enhances, rather than diminishes, the values that underpin artistic expression. Whether you're a professional designer, a marketer, or someone exploring your creative side, your choices in how you use AI tools will shape the future of this technology.

As we move forward, the path is clear: innovation and regulation must go hand in hand. By embracing both the opportunities and the responsibilities of AI, we can create a future where tools like Imagen 3 empower people to imagine and build without compromising ethics or integrity. The journey is just beginning, and it's one we're all a part of—exploring, shaping, and redefining the creative possibilities of tomorrow.

Conclusion

Imagen 3 stands as a testament to how far we've come in merging technology and creativity. From transforming simple text prompts into stunning visuals to redefining the workflows of professionals and hobbyists alike, its impact is nothing short of revolutionary. It has not only expanded what's possible in visual creation but has also made creativity accessible to anyone with an idea and the curiosity to explore.

The true power of Imagen 3 lies in its ability to enhance human creativity, not replace it. While AI handles the technical and repetitive aspects of creation, it's the human touch that guides the vision, emotion, and storytelling behind every project. This synergy between human imagination and AI precision represents a new frontier in creative expression, where the boundaries of what we can dream and achieve are constantly being pushed.

As we embrace tools like Imagen 3, it's essential to remember the responsibilities that come with them. Creativity is not just about making something new; it's about doing so with respect, fairness, and integrity. The ethical considerations surrounding AI-generated content—ownership, originality, and potential misuse—require thoughtfulness from both developers and users. By navigating these challenges carefully, we can ensure that AI remains a force for good in the creative world.

To those exploring Imagen 3 for the first time, let it be a gateway to experimentation and discovery. Try new prompts, push its limits, and let it spark ideas you didn't know you had. To seasoned professionals, let it be a partner that complements your skillset, helping you achieve more while staying true to your artistic vision. And to everyone, let it serve as a reminder of the endless possibilities when technology and creativity come together.

The journey of Imagen 3 and AI tools like it is just beginning. As the technology evolves, so too will the opportunities to imagine, create, and innovate. It's an exciting time to be a creator, and the future promises even more transformative tools that will continue to reshape how we bring our ideas to life. Let's step into this future with open minds, guided by creativity, curiosity, and responsibility, as we redefine what it means to create in a world where imagination has no limits.